A Sensitive Subject

Cammerron Baits

BookLeaf
Publishing

India | USA | UK

Made with ❤ on the BookLeaf Publishing Platform
www.bookleafpub.in
www.bookleafpub.com

Dedication

For my husband, Christian—
who gave me space to unravel, to feel,
and for doing the work with me to rebuild.
Your love has been my strength and my refuge,
proving that intimacy we share holds even the hardest
truths
and still choose to stay.

And for the family — biological or chosen — I've known,
and the ones I've lost to death, to distance, to adoption,
or to time.
Each of you, in your own way, taught me how to endure,
how to love, and how to find meaning in the ache of
becoming.
You are all pieces of the man I've grown to be,
and this book is, in its own way,
my way of coming home to you.

Preface

This book began as a need—not to explain my past, but to understand why I still feel it vibrating beneath my skin.

I've come to believe that sensitivity isn't fragility. It's a form of endurance—the quiet strength to keep feeling when the world teaches you not to, and in doing so, you become a survivor, not a victim.

My work centers on revealing the truth within trauma through transparent, emotionally intelligent conversation. In exploring these five central traumas, I approached each through that same compassionate lens. Each cycle of poems became a mirror: a way to acknowledge hardship, celebrate resilience, and trace a hopeful path forward on the road my tenacious spirit has paved.

Throughout "A Sensitive Subject", we move through five raw and vulnerable human experiences and the poetic forms chosen to frame them. This book explores 5 types of poems in 5 styles cycling through one after another each trauma receiving 4 poems. The eleventh poem, "Precipice" is their common ground and invites us to pause and breath before we continue, this is written in

its own 6th style as a *Visual Image* poem.Each poem
adds to what I call a human archive of endurance,
intimacy, and reclamation. not as categories of pain, but
as chapters of becoming

- **Addiction** (*extended metaphor*)
- **Loss** (*narrative*)
- **Murder** (*sonnet*)
- **Abuse** (*Villanelle*)
- **Infidelity** (*freeform*)

As poet, sensitivity specialist, theatrical professional, and
survivor, I work to transform what others silence into
something felt and shared. This book embraces
sensitivity as both rebellion and art—an act of defiance
against the life I could have fallen into, and a testament
to emotional intelligence as a creative force. Because of
the nature of this work, I want our exchange to be
consensual. What you're about to read is deeply
personal. Some pages may sting. Some may mirror your
own reflection. You are welcome to move through it in
one sitting or return to it slowly. Your choice matters.
This structure exists intentionally—to ensure that what
you read, you read with awareness, agency, and care.
Pause when you need to.
Return when you're ready.
You are safe here, even when the words ache.

My hope is that this act of healing becomes participatory —that by sharing these vulnerable moments, others who have lived similar stories might feel seen, heard, and less alone in the quiet spaces where pain often hides.

I've dedicated my work—on stage, in life, and on the page—to helping people hold difficult truths safely. These poems are my way of holding my own. Thank you for taking the time to share this with me.
If you've ever been told you're too much, too soft, too emotional, too sensitive—this book is for you.
May it remind each of us that our sensitivity is not the wound, but the scar that proves we survived.

Acknowledgements

This book exists because of the people who taught me that sensitivity is not a flaw, but a compass.

To those who stood beside me when silence felt safer — your courage to listen allowed me to speak.

To the mentors who modeled compassion through accountability, and the artists who showed me that pain can transform into purpose, thank you for helping me see beauty in the becoming.

To my chosen family — those who call, check in, and remind me that rest is also resilience — your love keeps me grounded.

And to every survivor who has ever questioned whether their story mattered: it does. You matter.

To my husband, Christian — thank you for holding space for me to explore some of our most intimate hardships, and for meeting that vulnerability with patience, humor, and grace. Your willingness to walk through the fire with me, not away from it, helped me process and heal safely. Because of you, our marriage and friendship is continuing to grow and become stronger than ever. You remind me daily that love, when tended with care, can be both refuge and renewal.

To the inaugural Sensitivity Specialist Certification Cohort of 2025 — thank you for building a community rooted in empathy, accountability, and artistry. Together, we are changing how stories are told and how truth is held.
Finally, to the reader: thank you for choosing to feel with me. Your willingness to bear witness turns these poems from confession into connection.

May we all continue to be sensitive subjects — unafraid to feel deeply, speak truthfully, and heal loudly.

1. Ding Dong Ditch

Remember back when we were kids,
the game of Ding Dong Ditch.
We would press—then run and scream—
then laugh, fall to our knees.
The biggest prank: "Guess who it is!"
But oh— the fun I thought I'd miss,
when no one *really* came to visit.

One day, I saw them coming.
This was the first time I screamed:
"Hey, I want to try!"
Oh my God, how nice!
They let me play!
Those ding dong ditchers— and me
A 12-year-old – just a little guy –
the newest lost boy in Neverland!

But we all grow up; I'm no longer a kid.
It's a new game now: this Ding Dong Ditch.
All it takes— a hard day, or a fight—
and I think I hear the bell...
Don't open the door to answer.
Sit—
In anxiety.

Oh fuck—

I hear them squeal.
They're pressing again—
And again—
And again—
And again—
Ding– Dong– Ditched!

They brought friends
to ring the bell,
and all scream back
and beg of me:
Please!
Come back to visit!

Now, I'm back in an empty room—
all but the cravings, quiet as a mouse.
The more I sit, the louder the bell—
the louder I yell internally.

No longer fun and games—
this is my personal,
self-inflicted hell.
I shake...
and shiver...

and go numb –
Fuck off, ding dong ditcher!
I don't want to play!
Not today.
I'm done.

2. Outsider

I see myself in every orphan's story—
neglected by choice or circumstance.
Driven by a desperate reach for love's glory,
the iridescent shimmer of a feeling
that now survives only in fragments
of memory.

The government gave me a home—
a workhouse fit for Oliver Twist:
a bed, a meal, companions I never chose,
and adults who counted checks
instead of children.

My circumstance gave birth
to an unresting optimism—
singing harmony to Annie's refrain:
"The sun'll come out tomorrow."
And still I wonder,
is this grin a smile,
or my jaw clenching the pain?

I fancy myself a poet like Ponyboy,
painting sunsets across a skyline
of gunpowder and bloodied alleyways.

Born with a heart that makes room
for those who need me
to carry their hurt with tender hands—
like Sodapop, who steadies his brothers,
or Daryl, the reluctant patriarch
life demanded.

I know it'd be easier to walk away—
to let the world harden what it can't hold.
But I keep working these hands and heart
to the bone,
searching for a home
where I can lay my worries down
beside a beautiful face
seen through the dust life's kicked up.

Yes, I am an outsider—
stoic, scarred,
ready to fight for the lucky few
I've let read the lines of this greasy heart.
I've held myself
when no one else would.

But at some point,
a boy questions his fate.
He longs to be a man built not from pain,
but from persistence—

5

to craft a home with the same tenacity
that once kept him alive.

So I smile, even when I'm still asking
where love hides tonight.
I'll build the roof,
the fire,
the safety in December's chill.
My words won't fade,
my hands won't rest—
because I made it out.

And I let you in.
We built this home
with our own two hands.
The orphan boy became a man
who refuses to surrender.

3. The Call (A Broken Sonnet)

The phone rang sharp—I answered to despair,
a tremor in my chest, "our friend is missing."
My mind refused the sense of muggy air,
as if the world itself were half-erasing.

The carpet worn—no ground beneath my feet,
Screeching silence between each shattered word.
Her laughter still alive, her joy complete,
yet something darker pressed a dream deferred.

The news snuffed hope—she wasn't just missing,
but gone, past pain, past breath I prayed she held.
Relief cut cruel: her body freed the cost,
Slamming a door no love could have compelled.

In my gut I knew she wouldn't come home.

4. Salt and Sear

Why is it always those you trust the most,
Love-bombs distract as they stalk your demons,
Your quaking heart, left haunted by their ghost.

A rose-colored fog of disillusion,
You only see good, a moth to their flame,
Convinced it is love, but it's confusion.

Because it's always those you trust the most,
Each strike disguised as devotion, as care,
The lamb led to slaughter, served up for roast.

The fire burns hot, then softens to deceive,
They season your wounds, then salt what they sear,
A feast of control you're forced to receive.

So now—who are those you can trust the most?
Starving for love, but flinching when it's near,
Each time you reach, *your* weakness diagnosed.

Why is it always those you trust the most,
Who shatter your spirit, leave you in pieces—
Needing an exorcist to free the host
From all your lies. You had me so engrossed.

5. Deserted

I've been walking in the desert
On a treadmill of sand,
moving me miles to end where we began.
Along the way we were separated.
Your sense of direction is much stronger,
so I tell myself you're safe
back at home,
while I still roam this desert
on my own.

Equipped with the tools to return to you
The compass, obstinate,
started pointing south days ago,
and today when I realized it,
the map disintegrated in my hands.
Without a marker to identify where we stand
We lost our way,
You left me burned.

Tangled in passing tumble weeds,
We're not dead yet.
On the horizon,
all visions of us:
raking the leaves of that big tree out front;

weeding our landscape to clear my path home.
Blink once,
we're there;
Blink twice,
I'm alone.

Did my heart see a damn mirage?
A brief image of who I truly want?
This heatwave mocks my desire!
I muster strength and run due north
Until I fall to my knees panting to catch my breath.

I found a river in the desert
that I can't drink:
it runs from my eyes.

My face stained,
my knees continue to bleed.
I pick myself up and begin again
longing to be engulfed
by the sun that burned me.

Every step brings me closer to us.

6. Clockwork (Ding)

You ask me, do I think of you?
Like you don't know the answer.
You conceived a torrid love affair
that spun me around so fast
I lost my balance,
falling right back into you.
It happened just like clockwork.

You found me hiding
in shadows of my own making—
a half-lit room of memory and aching.
My hopeless-romantic heart
beats beneath the bruises,
quiet but desperate,
searching for a pulse
that wasn't mine.

And *Ding!—*
You knew exactly where to press.
You studied the fracture lines,
learned how to sell me salvation
wrapped in the shape of my regrets.
I purchased every promise
because it sounded like healing.

Not that I was "worthy" of it.

Love happens when you least expect it.
Out of nowhere you appeared,
I ran to you.
A fall-fast-and-hard kind of love,
the romance of a pre-teen daydream
dealing in flirty looks.
You swept me off my feet.

Lost in your eyes,
my pupils dilated for lessons.
Never looking back,
you take my hand,
giving me a key
unlocking parts of me
to a world you promised we'd inhabit.

Alone in the time we spent—
a classic case of quantity over quality
overcome by loneliness.
No one stays forever.
I dip it in. Just like clockwork,
my synapses ignite to free me.

The centripetal force weakens,
and I'm kicked to the curb. *Ding!*

God, you think you're clever,
a thirst trap sent to hypnotize
me with your alluring smile. *Ding!*
You snap, leaving me alone and dehydrated.
I get back in your car, knowing where this ends—
desperate to feel alive while you bury me.

Last time I responded was toxic—
distracted isolation.
The cost – everything.
A mask of manufactured laughter
surrounded by strangers I call friends.
Signal low, I text an SOS. *Ding!*
Searching for something to rescue me.

I took the breakup hard—
cold sweats and sleepless nights
scrolling through memories
of someone else's life.
I look at my face in the mirror—
Who's that person looking back?
You took the light from me,
and replaced it with a party
that never stops.

I walked out on you ten years ago,
but I'm still unpacking bags

discovering love notes you left for me.
You come around like clockwork. *Ding!*
A text comes in from *Leave on Read*: "Miss me?"
I can change your name, but it's still you.
I'm thinking of you now.

Somehow you know when to text,
like you're stalking me.
A massive fight – some big life change—
And *Ding!*–
Sometimes, you appear in faces on the street.
I bump into you at the urinal sober, at a club.
It would be so easy for you to pick me up,
but the crash would be eternal.

You rush through every roadblock,
knowing where to find me.
Then suddenly, a barrage of texts:
Ding! Ding! Ding!
"Hey." "You up?" "God, you're sexy."
My phone vibrates so much,
you're trying to arouse me,
but I've learned your patterns.
Your words hold little weight now.
"Talk to me! I know you miss me."
I did, but we crashed too many times.

Recently, it's been nonstop—
in the silence there's the *Ding!*
The persistence is familiar;
you know how to turn me on—
sparkling affirmation—
you're a minute man.
Risk everything for an hour,
just to feel the fall?
No, I won't come over
to feel you on my tongue.

You come around like clockwork,
to shoot your shot.
This time my nose won't bleed.
I know every trick you've got.
You taught me everything I know.

Like clockwork, *Ding!*
I turn off my phone.

7. A Portrait Of My Mother

Biology births a magnetic pullI kept swearing would
never matter—but the more I learn where I come fromthe
more that promise mocks my feigned confidence.
For so long, all I had of youwas a portrait, drawn and
signed,a quiet gift of loveyour hand stretching across
time to mine.
When I first held it,this small piece you gave,the charcoal
lines reached out,as if a drawing could save me.
The strokes gather into a face—I've always known.Your
eyes echo inside mine mirror my brows and jawboneAs
if you grab my face Besos upon each cheek closing the
distance between us with only a mothers tender care.
Sometimes it feels like I could touch youthrough the
shapes your pencil found,and if you could, you'd touch
me back—blending charcoal memories,guiding me to
you.
I traveled to Madrid once.I saw you and I in every face-
like that portrait had stepped off the page,a testament
that I belong to you.
A portrait of my mother,fierce and torn.I can feel the
pain she carried—leaving me so I wouldn't be harmed.
I cannot just be a portrait,a sketch of love pressed flat on
paper.I want to hold the child a mother forfeits,to calm
their breaking rage.

Even so, I study the portrait you drew for meYour eyes long to give the loveThat I longed to receive.Your jaw clenches for the sufferingYou never overcame for me. The rage bursts through me,when I find the polaroid—A new perceptive your face in colorTelling stories I've never heard side by side— the portrait and the picturefill gaps I never knew existedAnd that moment the portrait suddenly is alive.

I see the mother I always wanted And cannot deny she is mineSo I'm caught in the middle—to reconnect or resign?I stare at the portrait and the pictureListening for my mother's mouth to tell me what I need.

8. Hometown

I listen close— not for the blood, but why;
the moment when her light was choked away.
Each retold death, a haunting lullaby,
a way to name the ghosts that never stay.

I trace each clue like stitching open scars,
dreaming the wound might whisper back a truth.
My mind replays the crime, in quiet fright,
to summon the peace stolen by that night.

For those who've known the silence of the call,
The broadcast hum becomes familiar prayer—
To map the chaos, understand it all,
reclaim control from life's most cruel affair.

I do not crave the gore, but seek release,
for knowing justice never feels complete.

9. Show Must Go On (I Vanish)

Lights. Camera. Action. Flashback appears.
Show must go on, accept violation
entitled to own my talent and fears.

Power was slung like a whip through the tiers
Proving I have no say in what happens.
Lights. Camera. Action. Flashback appears.

Spotlight. I'm alone on the casting couch.
"Sit" take direction no chance to react;
Walk in tall, leave barely able to slouch

Think you're safe— "man" — they also prey on queers.
Mentors violate my naïveté.
Lights. Camera. Action. Flashback appears.

Petrified, right on cue, as they all watched
Unashamed, you do it in the open,
Naked, you grabbed my— inhibition squashed!

Sacrificed so much to work in this fear
is the dream worth the displayed attention?

Lights. Camera. Action. Flashback appears.
Lights. Camera. Action. And I Vanish.

10. Short Loin

I'm feeling
      Isolated
           alone
A short loin steak
meat chewed off the bone.
life was juicy as could be
months of betrayal
taking bites
        out of
          me.
Scarf it down without a thought,
He did all of that
for what?

He thought
He could
      have it all
         me in our bed
looking for holes in the wall
coming back to me each and every night
smiling in my face
looking for dudes
on a site

I tried to reconcile
how it all went down.
the man of my dreams
acting
     like a clown .
He's in there
somewhere
way
   deep
         down.
He got lost
not forgotten

he can be found!

Not willing
to stop the fight
I'll keep throwing punches with cloudy eyes,

K.O!

.

Lights
   Out

Putting me to bed at night.

I have to know
He'll be at my side.
With me on the walk
There in the ring.
Fighting.
        for a spot.
fighting.
        on the same team.

We had
everything we wanted.
We were living in the dream
now when I go to bed at night
all I do is
            scream.
I know
I just have to breathe
each inhale more suffocating.
I'm feeling isolated
and alone
like a short loin steak,
meat chewed off the bone.

all this happened
because he felt the same .

Unable to communicate
what he needs.

.

so your appetite grew

hungry

curiosity to feed.

I don't want to be the same.
Repeat the mistakes
walk away from the dream.

It's not too late.

We need to cook a little longer
He cut into me
all I do is

bleed...

11. Precipice

you know the feeling when time
stands still chaos engulfs and
you freeze with joy or surprise
good bad a moment you die
you gasp unable to breathe
heart stops a vein of sand
one grain on the edge
it hangs
frozen
until it drops
punches you clean
at once both face and gut
hearts pounding intensifies
the moment on the edge brief
the impact changes everything
still you embrace determination
pray to survive the sands of time

12. Splash Zone

I take a seat at the front of the toboggan,
feeling like a winner just to experience the ride.
I stood in line for hours— how lucky, I thought —
to be here for this wild descent.

Children laugh,
their joy drowning the shrill of grown men's screams.
The promise is simple—
a rush of adrenaline,
a drop that makes our stomachs flip.
The sun catching droplets mid air
Turning anticipation into golden exhilaration.
They call it *Splash Mountain.*

Eagerly, I buckle in—
hands and arms inside at all times—
and brace myself for the plunge.
My heart counts down faster than the clock.
The wheels release,
gravity takes the lead,
and I realize too late—
this ride ends in a flood.

They don't warn you how

choices you make are not yours alone.
How water carries more than thrill—
it carries every wide-eyed dream,
every ripple of destruction,
Downstream.

I thought I was safe,
wrapped in my poncho of denial,
believing love could keep me dry.
But addiction doesn't stay in its lane—
it sprays,
it stains,
it soaks
through every surface.

I watched wave after wave
crash over the people I love—
the rows behind me,
onlookers who never chose this ride.
I looked back and saw their eyes
salt-stung,
their laughter washed away.
How soaked they were—
how small I was—
as I slink off the ride,
red-eyed, alone, and
soaked.

It's called *the splash zone*,
as if proximity were consent,
as if we all signed up for the flood.
But no one tells you—
even when you aren't the one drowning,
you can still choke on the aftermath.

And somewhere—
someone still stands in line,
ticket in hand,
smiling at the promise of the drop.

They don't see the puddles
left by those before them,
don't hear the quiet sobs
beneath the sound of rushing water.
They only feel the thrill.

They don't yet know—
every ride ends wet,
and the splash never hits
just one.

13. Time Capsule

He kneels beneath the oak, a shoebox waiting—
the cardboard patter of a heart learning to archive itself.

First, two CDs.
One replays in his mind—"Pretty Little Adriana,"
the song that gave his sister her name,
a childhood favorite that built a bond
before she was even born.
The other, "Young the Giant's" first album—
the chords that bound him and his sister
through speakers, concerts and distance,
where harmony meant home, friendship, family—
all in one.

Next, a karaoke mic—
the same one he carried down his grandmother's street,
touring porches and driveways like small stages.
She'd clap from a distance, eyes shining,
as he learned how joy could echo back power,
how a song could be weapon, armor, strength—
all the same.

He tenderly places a Phoenix,
the sculpture he built with his mother

for a school project of recycled dreams.
Wire hangers and feathers,
foam and fingerprints—
her raccoon spirit guiding his hands,
showing him that rebirth can be made
when you honor your creative gift.

Then, a soccer trophy.
Its dull brass—plastic, really—
remembers his years playing:
Encouraging grass-stained knees,
a goal that made his father cheer.
Fractured bones, repair to form a son his father shaped
I see the impact as though he can feel that hand
on his shoulder—steady, watchful—
the quiet promise of a father's guidance
that outlives applause.

Two degrees follow—proof
that curiosity is its own resurrection.
Paper seals of persistence,
his mind stretched wide enough to hold
every version of himself.
Validation of a dream fulfilled—
milestones carved along his climb.

He adds a Polaroid of our first home—

the one we found after endless turns
through a city that did not yet know our names.
We stood on the curb, shaded by this same oak,
and felt the light through the windows,
knowing this was where we'd grow roots.

Finally, our rings—
promises intertwined within our fingers,
as we hold hands nested together like twin moons.
Now too small to wear,
but they've witnessed every chapter
of our perfectly imperfect love story.
They gleam without weight—
commitment and safety shaped
into something as natural as breath.
We exchange continued promises
till the end of our days,
and with a kiss, place our old rings in,
grateful for the decades they've seen us through.

He buries the box gently,
patting the soil flat—meticulous,
as if pressing pause on time.
"This is who I am," he whispers.
"If I forget, please dig here to remind me."
I want to promise he never will forget,
but instead I hold him close and say,

"I'll remind you every day of our lives."

Time stops in our embrace,
I trace the lines of his hand like constellations—
mapping the sky I'd be lost without.
He grounds me, roots me,
the compass I never learned to read.
I fear the day I wake and he's gone—
to mind, or to morning—
I'd lose my gravity.

He laughs it off, but I hear the tremor.
It isn't death he fears, but erasure—
the theft of self that leaves the body.
The most intelligent man I have ever known,
too sharp for his own good—
his brilliant mind becomes his biggest fear:
that he might lose himself
when he loses his mind.

He is so keen, so present,
I cannot picture a world where he fades.
Even if memory unravels,
I'll keep the thread taut between us.
He nods, eyes on the tree's trunk,
counting the years like shovelfuls.

"Someday," he says,
"if I forget your name,
open the box beneath the roots.
Remind me that we were infinite—
that love, when deep enough,
doesn't rot—
it roots."

14. Tethered

I clutch your voice between my trembling hands,
The weight of blue crystal beckons your name.
I regain my breath where our hearts once planned.
Your silver whispers set my heart aflame.

Swift circles stir the air gifting relief;
the chain, our tether bonding loss to kin.
"Yes" confirms instinct, you support and breathe.
"No" — a redirection born within me.

The pendulum speaks with your clarity.
Honest, definitive divination
pulls me to move with your dexterity.
Solace erased my heart's palpitation.

I ask — you answer. Stillness breaks apart.
The chain swings wild — your pulse beneath my heart.

15. Stalled

How quickly things you have never noticed
become the moments you never forget.
Went in without a thought and then left pissed.

My knees still shake from what my body met,
crammed, cold against the stall, door locked, I froze—
became the moment I'll never forget.

I pulled up my shorts, hands still shaking slow,
the floor took notes on what my mind blacked out,
neon lights now dim with looming shadow.

I cursed that stall, its walls still holding show,
of men who take and assume consent—
those are the moments I'll never forget.

Lights flicker—memory floods, uninvited.
I steady my breath, refuse to look away.
How quickly things I have never noticed
become the moments I'll never forget.

16. The Storm

The storm will destroy what isn't solid,
yet it will reveal what truly is.
I hesitate to disembark the plane
carrying twice as much baggage
than when I left home,
unsure if home is even
what I'll see
when I return.

You pull up to take me back
and yet it's like you are
cosplaying my husband.
I don't recognize you.
Reality chokes me,
and I brace for impact.

Questions race
at an Olympic speed
in my mind,
each one competing to be
the one I ask.
Never stopping
like their lives depend on it—
and maybe they do—

and maybe ours does too?

A rare moment when I censor myself,
I'm guarded:
not wanting to say the wrong thing
scared it will be the gust of wind
to knock down the framing,
every plate and stud that holds our home together,
unsure just how stable we are.

The need for answers tests the limits of my desire
to contain what I am desperate to know.
Then, out squeaks the one-word question
I may never fully know the answer to,
"Why?"

You reach for my hand, I don't want to.

Hard conversations
Lingering—
Doubts,
fights,
insecurity,
patience,
hard work,
consistency—
and I look around.

The storm is gone.
Us inside the still-standing house
Not without its damage.

You reach for my hand, and I want to

The storm will destroy what isn't solid,
Yet it will reveal what truly is.
It left us exposed to the natural elements
Ripped holes in walls
we spent hours painting,
Cracked windows
I hadn't realized needed replacing,
But the foundation
is as solid as it's ever been.
Perfect bones to rebuild
a perfect home.

You reach for my hand, and I need to

So I do. I hold it,
and all that I felt
the first time we interlocked our fingers
bubbles to the surface
And what's this?
safety?
I've missed you...

I look back at you,
at your normal clothes,
and I recognize you again,
This man I know.

We begin to sift through
what we can salvage,
and for the first time
since the storm
I know the marriage.

17. Cold Turkey

My mentor sat me down to eat.
Said, "let's talk about what's left over."
She pulled the turkey from the fridge—
cold slabs sweating through plastic skin,
a body she meant to reheat.

Steam rose like club nights of old highs.
The smell—salt and sweet decay—
clung to my lungs,
reminding me how craving wears no face.

She served me a meal of thanksgiving:
all the talent she's seen leak from my pores,
the heart I offer others—gravy, thick and golden—
poured over a mountain
of mashed potatoes,
grainy with lies,
still hot with deceit.
She tells me, "you still have a feast in front of you."

But I can't taste the thanks.
Every bite feels like penance.
The turkey stares back, pale with withdrawal,
flesh trembling in the heat.

I chew slowly,
afraid my jaw might remember the grind.

The reality: this could be my last meal
if I don't take the love she offers.
I butter my bread with precision,
desperate to fill the hollowness.
She refills my cup;
I mistake the water for mercy.

Her eyes glisten—
a reflection of the ache in mine.
The plea sits unspoken:
save me before I lose myself again—please.
Water spills,
soaking through denim,
darkening my lap
 with the weight of what's left unsaid.
The air thickens,
time stops.
The wind whistles its warning—
"This could be your last thanksgiving."

I move the peas and carrots
in pointless choreography,
as if arranging my regrets.
Hours pass as she fights

for the right words to get through.
I shift in my seat without words
to assure her—they have.

Only the turkey remains,
sweating harder than I am.
Unappetizing, but necessary—
protein to keep me from disappearing.
Each swallow burns like confession.
The meat clings to my teeth,
the flavor—metallic,
like a nosebleed at 4 a.m.

A contradiction, she calls it—
"strength inside the shaking."
But all I feel is fever—
and the breaking.
The room spins slow,
my body is a defrosting carcass.
I hear her voice, but only the echo:
"You can live on what's left."

I sit before the empty plate—
hands trembling,
tears saltier than gravy.
November outside presses its cold mouth to the window.
The turkey in my stomach turns.

I whisper thanks,
swallowing courage
like the last bite I'll ever keep down.

Years later, we've lost contact—
but not our connection.
We no longer share meals together,
but each year I still think of her and give thanks
for that cold turkey—
she saved me.

18. The Roaches (In 2 Parts)

I - In the Dark

There are weeks when I've been breathing,
though I can't explain how.
It feels as if my head's been cut clean off—
a guillotine of memory severing thought from body.
You'd think I would bleed out,
collapse in some dramatic, cinematic end.

But no—
the lungs keep moving.
The chest still rises, shallow but certain,
as if air has found another way in.
Life cheats through secret spiracles,
tiny holes along my ribs
where instinct gasps when reason can't.

Somewhere between panic and evolution,
I've learned to survive like this—
to detach what hurts too much to feel,
to let the nervous system go silent
so the rest of me can continue crawling.

My blood forgets the luxury of a pulse.

My heart learns to whisper without instruction.
I am a miracle of malfunction,
a breathing body without a head,
still navigating the dark.
Instead, I evolve—
my spine morphs into a hinge,
learning to bend, to fold myself down
to something manageable, palatable,
a creature of corners and survival.

My skin hardens—not calloused, but engineered,
a shell that keeps the soft parts hidden.
It glistens under pressure,
a lacquer of endurance grown cell by cell.
You can't tell where the armor ends
and the body begins.

Inside, I hum.
A silent machine, self-repairing.
No bones to break—just panels that shift and seal.
Pain ricochets off the surface;
fear slides down the ridges and drains into the cracks.
This is not invincibility—
it's memory calcified.

When pain hunts me,
I scatter,

splitting into fragments of motion,
each piece remembering how to live without the rest.
My ghosts never keep up;
they're too slow, too sentimental.
I leave them behind like discarded molts—
husks of who I was before survival taught me better.

Sometimes I think I'm not human—
just a cockroach,
built to live where nothing should.
To eat dust, to wear ruin like perfume,
to be despised and still remain.

But then I met you—
and you had wings.
Not the kind born of luck or lineage,
but ones grown from the rot—
from the corners where we were left to hide.

We come from the same dark—
the same walls that tried to seal us in.
But somehow, we learned to climb them,
to rise from the fostered dust,
to turn the shame they fed us
into something that glitters
midair.

You remind me survival doesn't have to crawl.
It can take flight.
It can be beautiful.

II – We Evolve

It happened in a strange town—
rain hammering down like confession.
We were looking for forgotten things—
antiques,
stories trapped behind a glass locked door,
refusing to be read.

My hair soaked to its roots,
a Chia pet of nerves and uncertainty,
I ducked into a barbershop
where your coworker waved me in.
I almost didn't.
My kind of hair,
my kind of history—
not everyone knows how to hold either.

Then I turned,
and there you were—
curls mirroring mine,

a face that made my ribs ache,
an intuition pushing me to poke my head
out of the cracks and venture into the light,
through the piercing hiss of my aching heart.
You said, "You're safe with me,"
and I believed you.

We talked—
about DNA tests and tangled bloodlines,
about families drawn in pencil
and erased by strangers.
Each word we shared
tightened a thread
I didn't know was attached.

You trimmed the edges of my hair—
as if you were trimming grief.
And when I looked up,
I saw my mother in your eyes.

You confessed you were a cockroach.
I laughed—
said we both are,
but with wings.
We laughed again,
half afraid of what that meant,
half desperate to believe it.

In the car, my husband whispered,
"Hey mister—did we just meet your sister?"
And I didn't know.
But for the first time,
I didn't feel alone.

Later, scrolling through your photos—
your smile, your ease,
the way you hold space for your own survival—
I thought of us— two insects of resilience,
cracked but not crushed,
still crawling through the dark—
except now, we both have
wings.

I imagine a tattoo, I'll get
of a cockroach with wings
Not for family confirmed,
but the one I felt—
the one that looked back in the mirror
and saw me.

Not human.
Not broken.
But a cockroach
with wings.

19. A Sonnet for the Sunflowers

You were the sunlight in the storm we knew,
A soul that made the darkest corners glow.
Like sunflowers, your presence warmed us through,
Your laughter planting seeds we still let grow.

The world was cruel, it tried to steal your flame,
But light like yours refuses to be gone.
I see your smile each time I hear your name,
It breaks the night and calls me to move on.

Your "joie de vivre" shines for infinity,
The way we miss you cuts but also heals.
Your french horn blares bright, and free Memories—
A force the shadow never can conceal.

So bloom in me, my friend, though you are gone,
Your light lives on each time I face the dawn.

20. Handsome

All my life—I've been told I was handsome,
they would say, "At least you are beautiful"
I claimed their words in who I would become.

Their want was hunger, frozen I succumb,
took what they pleased, relinquished my control.
All my life—I've been told I was handsome.

I learned to smile though every nerve went numb,
while silence wrapped its hands around my soul.
All my life—I've been told I was handsome.

Then came a love that called me to come home,
who touched the truth beneath the role.
He found worth in who I had now become.

He saw the calm that years of pain had won,
now peace replaces what once burned ember.
All my life—I've been told I was handsome,
I found my worth in who I've now become.

21. A Perfect Day

Does the perfect day exist? I truly think he'd say,
"how do we define that? Perfect in which way?

Perfect for me? Perfect for us? Perfect for who?
Perfect in emotional sway, or in the things we do?"

I think for it to be perfect, no worries could live there:
no self-doubt or depression; no anxiety; no despair.

To have a day be perfect he needs to know his worth
To know his heart burns brightly enough to light the
Earth.

He'd have to accept my love with outstretched open
arms
To feel worthy to receive it and not sound the alarms.

It wouldn't be a work day with obligations to stress him
out
Surrounded by his loved ones either home or out about.

At home, the TV wraps us in cuddles with the pup
We cook or craft whatever our imagination whips up.

When out, he'd want his camera, a reminder of the joy that brings
Exploring new perspectives, sharing how we see things.

If our friends were visiting, he'd love to share our life,
the home that we've created, and places we go at night.

To be fair, I don't know If the perfect day existed,
Entangled in our lives, would we accidentally miss it?

Not to sound existential or add temporary dread,
But for it to be perfect, first we'd need to leave our head.

Though if there's one thing I could dream for this man of mine
It's in the imperfection he takes one day at a time;

He learns to smile at the small things like when we first met
To laugh and joke and be a fool. Forget stress and regret.

And I know you didn't ask what a perfect day was for me?
A day in the life— just like now— is exactly what I see.

It's the two of us together, Holding hands day by day
taking life as a team, whatever comes our way.

A perfect day for me is simply knowing that you're here;
that we're building it together; that I've nothing left to
fear

That's what makes it all so easy, our marriage and our
vow:
Its perfection lies in living the life we dream together
now.

Cover Artwork Acknowledgement

Cover artwork and photography
by Cammerron Baits.

The collage is composed from photographs taken during
his trip to Madrid—an experience reflected in the poem
"A Portrait of My Mother." The piece stands as
Cammerron's own self-portrait, combining fragments of
his experience on that trip to mirror the many fractured
pieces of his story. Together, they invite the viewer to
look him in the eyes and see through to the heart and
soul of the man behind the poetry—he becomes the
sensitive subject. This cover holds those fragments close,
just as the book does—honoring where the story has
been, and leaving space for what's still becoming.

www.ingramcontent.com/pod-product-compliance
Lightning Source LLC
Chambersburg PA
CBHW060353050426

42449CB00011B/2962